Major US Historical Wars

THE CIVIL WAR

Samuel W. Crompton

Mason Crest
Philadelphia

Mason Crest
450 Parkway Drive, Suite D
Broomall, PA 19008
www.masoncrest.com

Printed and bound in the United States of America.
CPSIA Compliance Information: Batch #MUW2015.
For further information, contact Mason Crest at 1-866-MCP-Book.

3 5 7 9 8 6 4 2
Library of Congress Cataloging-in-Publication Data

ISBN: 978-1-4222-3354-2 (hc)
ISBN: 978-1-4222-8594-7 (ebook)

Major US Historical Wars series ISBN: 978-1-4222-3352-8

Picture Credits: Library of Congress: 1, 7, 11, 14, 17, 19, 21, 22, 29, 35, 38, 40, 42, 44, 51, 54, 59; National Archives: 18, 31, 33, 39, 47, 50; National Guard Heritage Collection: 27, 49; Photos.com: 9; used under license from Shutterstock, Inc.: 13, 24.

About the Author: Samuel Willard Crompton began play-acting the battles of the Civil War in his teenage years. Today he is a historian, teaching at Holyoke Community College and writing books for different audiences. His most recent publication is the *Handy Civil War Answer Book*, published in 2014.

TABLE OF CONTENTS

KEY ICONS TO LOOK FOR:

Text-dependent questions: These questions send the reader back to the text for more careful attention to the evidence presented there.

Words to understand: These words with their easy-to-understand definitions will increase the reader's understanding of the text, while building vocabulary skills.

Series glossary of key terms: This back-of-the book glossary contains terminology used throughout this series. Words found here increase the reader's ability to read and comprehend higher-level books and articles in this field.

Research projects: Readers are pointed toward areas of further inquiry connected to each chapter. Suggestions are provided for projects that encourage deeper research and analysis.

Sidebars: This boxed material within the main text allows readers to build knowledge, gain insights, explore possibilities, and broaden their perspectives by weaving together additional information to provide realistic and holistic perspectives.

Other Titles in This Series

Introduction

by Series Consultant
Jason Musteen

Why should middle and high school students read about and study American wars? Does doing so promote militarism or instill misguided patriotism? The United States of America was born at war, and the nation has spent the majority of its existence at war. Our wars have demonstrated both the best and worst of who we are. They have freed millions from oppression and slavery, but they have also been a vehicle for fear, racism, and imperialism. Warfare has shaped the geography of our nation, informed our laws, and it even inspired our national anthem. It has united us and it has divided us.

Lt. Col. Jason R. Musteen is a U.S. Army Cavalry officer and combat veteran who has held various command and staff jobs in Infantry and Cavalry units. He holds a PhD in Napoleonic History from Florida State University and currently serves as Chief of the Division of Military History at the U.S. Military Academy at West Point. He has appeared frequently on the History Channel.

Valley Forge, the *USS Constitution*, Gettysburg, Wounded Knee, Belleau Wood, Normandy, Midway, Inchon, the A Shau Valley, and Fallujah are all a part of who we are as a nation. Therefore, the study of America at war does not necessarily make students or educators militaristic; rather, it makes them thorough and responsible. To ignore warfare, which has been such a significant part of our history, would not only leave our education incomplete, it would also be negligent.

For those who wish to avoid warfare, or to at least limit its horrors, understanding conflict is a worthwhile, and even necessary, pursuit. The American author John Steinbeck once said, "all war is a symptom of man's failure as a thinking animal." If Steinbeck is right, then we must think.

And we must think about war. We must study war with all its attendant horrors and miseries. We must study the heroes and the villains. We must study the root causes of our wars, how we chose to fight them, and what has been achieved or lost through them. The study of America at war is an essential component of being an educated American.

Still, there is something compelling in our military history that makes the study not only necessary, but enjoyable, as well. The desperation that drove Washington's soldiers across the Delaware River at the end of 1776 intensifies an exciting story of American success against all odds. The sailors and Marines who planted the American flag on the rocky peak of Mount Suribachi on Iwo Jima still speak to us of courage and sacrifice. The commitment that led American airmen to the relief of West Berlin in the Cold War inspires us to the service of others. The stories of these men and women are exciting, and they matter. We should study them. Moreover, for all the suffering it brings, war has at times served noble purposes for the United States. Americans can find common pride in the chronicle of the Continental Army's few victories and many defeats in the struggle for independence. We can accept that despite inflicting deep national wounds and lingering division, our Civil War yielded admirable results in the abolition of slavery and eventual national unity. We can celebrate American resolve and character as the nation rallied behind a common cause to free the world from tyranny in World War II. We can do all that without necessarily promoting war.

In this series of books, Mason Crest Publishers offers students a foundation for the study of American wars. Building on the expertise of a team of accomplished authors, the series explores the causes, conduct, and consequences of America's wars. It also presents educators with the means to take their students to a deeper understanding of the material through additional research and project ideas. I commend it to all students and to those who educate them to become responsible, informed Americans.

Chapter 1:

THE CIVIL WAR BEGINS

T housands of people in the city of Charleston, South Carolina, stayed up all night on April 11, 1861. They knew that the crisis, which had been building for so long, was about to erupt.

At about 4:15 A.M., on April 12, a single cannon shell flew from the mouth of a Confederate cannon. This shell made a long arc and then crashed against the wall of Fort Sumter, a federal military installation on an island in the harbor. No one was hurt, but that cannon shot started the American Civil War.

This 19th century artwork depicts the Confederate bombardment of Fort Sumter that began on April 12, 1861.

WORDS TO UNDERSTAND IN THIS CHAPTER

An *abolitionist* believes in the complete eradication of slavery. Many Northerners were lukewarm abolitionists, meaning they preferred to let Southerners see the error of their ways in time, rather than forcing the issue.

A *rostrum* is very similar to a podium, meaning that it serves as the place where the speaker stands. The word itself comes to us from ancient Rome.

The *Union* has meant many things through the years, but it essentially refers to the union, or compact between, the original 13 states, which, over time, grew to include all 50.

The Union garrison did not respond at once. They waited until morning provided better light, and then they answered with guns of their own. A ferocious bombardment followed. After 24 hours of cannon fire, Union Major Robert Anderson agreed to surrender Fort Sumter. The flag of the United States was pulled down, and troops from the small federal garrison were evacuated, by steamship, to New York City.

Casualties had been very low, but no one was deceived about the meaning of the assault. Once a foe—even one who spoke the same language—fired on the flag of the United States, the American people would respond. And the first powerful demonstration of this fact took place eight days after that cannon shot at Fort Sumter. On April 20, 1861, nearly 200,000 people thronged the streets of Manhattan. One speaker after another went to the *rostrum* to proclaim his belief in, and love for, the United States.

Constitution and Compromise

The U.S. Constitution is a document, adopted by the states in 1787, that sets out the framework for government in the United States. When the Constitution was written in Philadelphia during the summer of 1787, its authors tried to skirt the issue of slavery. They recognized that slavery could potentially divide the Northern and Southern states—something they wished to avoid. However, one thing they could not avoid was the matter of representation in Congress's House of Representatives, which was determined by population. Southern states wanted slaves counted as part of their populations; Northern states argued that since the slaves did not have the rights of citizens, they should not be included in the population count. In the end, the delegates agreed that each African-American slave would count as three-fifths of a person for the purpose of the census. This compromise, and others, preserved peace between the Northern and Southern states for many years.

In 1818, when the Missouri Territory asked to be considered for statehood, some Northern leaders wanted slavery to be illegal there. At the time there were an equal number of slave and nonslave states, and political leaders did not want to upset the balance between them. The controversy was settled when Maine broke away from Massachusetts and was admitted to the *Union* as a free state at the same time that Missouri entered the Union as a slave state.

It was then proposed that no more slave states would be created from territories north of Missouri's southern border. Congress passed this proposal, which came to be known as the Missouri Compromise. Along with the practice of admitting states in pairs—one slave, one

Slaves pick cotton on a Southern plantation, 1850s. On the eve of the Civil War, nearly 4 million African Americans were held in slavery in the 15 states where the institution was permitted. Their labor fueled the South's economy, which was based on farming.

free—in order to maintain the balance of power in the U.S. Senate, the Missouri Compromise was a guiding principle of national politics for more than 30 years.

The Compromise of 1850

In 1850, California applied for entry to the Union as a free state. Months of debate and contention followed. In the fall of 1850, Congress approved a series of bills that collectively became known as the Compromise of 1850. Under its provisions, California did enter as a free state, and the Territories of Utah and New Mexico were created. At the same time, Congress enacted a new Fugitive Slave Law. This law required sheriffs and constables in Northern states to help Southerners capture escaped slaves and return them to the plantations.

Southern efforts to enforce the Fugitive Slave Law led to anger and bitterness between slave states and nonslave states. Harriet Beecher Stowe's novel *Uncle Tom's Cabin*, published in 1852, opened the eyes of many Northerners to the horrors of slavery. Southerners, meanwhile, felt increasingly under attack from their Northern compatriots.

In 1859, a Northern *abolitionist* by the name of John Brown, seized the federal armory at Harpers Ferry, Virginia. Brown wanted to incite a slave rebellion. He even had 2,500 wooden pikes manufactured, which he intended to distribute among the slaves. Brown failed, however, and was captured, tried, and sentenced to death.

Seldom has a failed attempt been so successful in the long run. Brown went to his death, in December 1859, without a word of complaint or anger. His noble conduct in the days before his execution persuaded thousands, perhaps hundreds of thousands, of Northerners that he was in the right. An equal number of Southerners were convinced that the North had no sympathy for their way of life, and that if Brown had freed the slaves, those slaves would have murdered the slaveowners in their sleep.

The Election of 1860

In 1860, Abraham Lincoln of Illinois won the Republican nomination. The Democratic Party split into two groups, with the Northern Democrats nominating Stephen A. Douglas and the Southern Democrats nominating John C. Breckinridge. There was even a third party, the Constitutional Union, spearheaded by John Bell.

Since there were four parties contending for votes, it is not surprising that Lincoln and his vice-presidential candidate, Hannibal Hamlin, won the election of 1860. What is surprising is that so many Southerners regarded Lincoln as their sworn enemy. Although Lincoln was opposed to slavery, he had no plans to make it illegal or impose any restrictions on it when he took office. Lincoln believed that the states would have to decide to end slavery, not the federal government.

Even before Lincoln was sworn into office, South Carolina declared that it would secede from the Union. This action was taken in Charleston on December 20, 1860.

Lincoln came into office on March 4, 1861, determined to

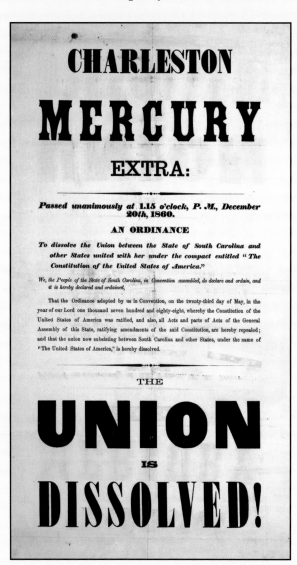

A South Carolina newspaper announces the state's secession from the United States, December 20, 1860. Four months later, the Civil War would begin with an artillery bombardment in Charleston harbor.

hold the nation together. The people of Charleston, on the other hand, were determined to break the nation apart. On April 12, 1861, the guns spoke for the first time, and the Civil War began.

The First Battle

The first skirmishes were fought in and around Washington, D.C., but the first real battle came on July 21, 1861. Union General Irwin McDowell brought 35,000 federal troops out of Washington and across the Virginia countryside. He was met by Confederate Generals Pierre G. T. Beauregard and Joseph E. Johnston, leading an equal number of Southern troops. The North called it the Battle of Bull Run, after a stream that meandered between the positions of the two armies. The South named it the Battle of Manassas, after an important railway junction that was close by.

On July 21, 1861, the day of the First Battle of Bull Run/Manassas, it was intensely hot in northern Virginia. The men on both sides carried heavy equipment. Even worse, they were nearly blinded, temporarily, by the smoke coming from gun cartridges. Though there were not many trained soldiers on either side, both sides fought with great determination and intensity.

Confederate Brigadier-General Thomas Jackson earned his famous nickname during that battle. A fellow Confederate general, seeking to encourage his men, shouted, "Look men! There stands Jackson like a stone wall! Rally behind the Virginians!"

Stonewall Jackson's determination in the face of the enemy encouraged the other Confederates, and by midafternoon the Union soldiers

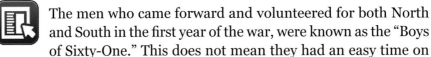

The men who came forward and volunteered for both North and South in the first year of the war, were known as the "Boys of Sixty-One." This does not mean they had an easy time on the battlefield, however.

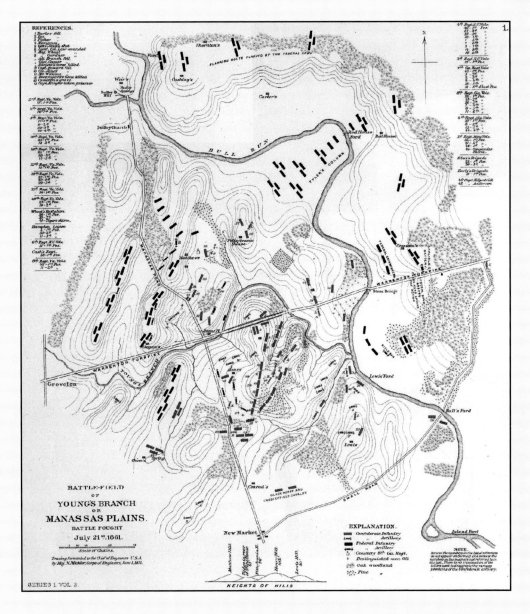

Map of the battlefield at Manassas, showing the Union armies (in blue) and the Confederate forces (in red).

were retreating, some in an orderly fashion; others fleeing. There were pileups of soldiers, horses, and even carriages. Most of the Union forces reached Washington, D.C. They had been trounced.

President Jefferson Davis arrived on the battlefield late in the day. He put out a call for victory celebrations, acting as if the war had already been

In July 1861, the Union and Confederate armies clashed near Manassas Junction, Virginia. Union leaders had confidently expected an easy victory, but the Confederates fought hard and routed the inexperienced federal troops.

won. He was mistaken. The heat, the smoke, and the confusion were all indications of what the war would become: a terrible meat-grinder.

The Two Theaters

Right from the beginning, there were two theaters in the Civil War. The Eastern Theater centered on the 110 miles (177km) of countryside between

Washington, D.C. and Richmond, Virginia. The Western Theater was much longer, and broader. It ran from Bowling Green, Kentucky all the way to the Mississippi River.

The Union held several key advantages in the Western Theater. The greater room, or geographic space, meant that the North could deploy its larger number of troops to good effect. Then, too, the Union had better, more inspiring generals in the West than its Confederate opponents did. One of these generals was Ulysses S. Grant.

Born in Ohio in 1822, Grant was 39 when the war began. After a successful Army career in the Mexican-American War (1846–1848), Grant became a drifter, failing at one occupation after another. All this changed when the Civil War broke out. Grant suddenly gained a purpose in life. Volunteering for the Army, he quickly rose to colonel, and then brigadier-general.

In the late summer of 1861, Grant and his men occupied the little town of Cairo, Illinois, located where the Ohio and Mississippi Rivers come together. By holding this vital junction point, Grant ensured that the Union would have an advantage in the Western Theater. He also made a name for himself, and this would eventually propel him to the highest rank in the military.

The International Situation

One of the greatest hopes of the Confederacy was that England, France, or perhaps both of them, would forge an alliance with the South. The Confederates had reason to believe these European nations would support their cause. Many members of the upper class in England and France did favor the Confederacy. And if ever there was a time when these European powers leaned toward the Confederacy, it was in December 1861.

A Union naval commander seized the British mail steamer *Trent*, and brought two Confederate envoys who were onboard—former U.S. Senators John Slidell of Louisiana and James Mason of Virginia—as prisoners to Boston. This sparked an international crisis, with thousands of British citizens furious about this insult to their national honor. For several weeks it seemed as if the Union might have to fight both England and the Confederacy. President Lincoln stepped in, however. The Confederate envoys were freed, and the anger on the other side of the Atlantic subsided. The Trent Affair was remembered for a long time afterward, however. It was a warning to the Union to carry on one fight at a time.

The End of the First Year

By the end of 1861, both the North and the South realized they had underestimated the other. The North had far more industrial power and a larger population, but the South had great fighting spirit. Those who had believed that the war would be short and swift now understood their mistake.

TEXT-DEPENDENT QUESTIONS

1. Which side won the bombardment of Fort Sumter?
2. At what battle did Thomas Jackson earn his famous nickname?
3. Which foreign country or countries might have intervened in the Civil War in 1861?

RESEARCH PROJECT

Photocopy the Stars and Stripes, the Stars and Bars (the Confederate flag), and the Union Jack of Great Britain. Put the three together in front of you, and write a short essay about the similarities and differences between them. What, for example, do the stars stand for? And what do the different crosses in the Union Jack mean?

Chapter 2

THE YEAR OF EMANCIPATION

During previous American wars—notably the Revolutionary War—most of the action had taken place in warm weather. Compared to earlier conflicts, the Civil War was conducted throughout the year.

Grant in the West

Ulysses S. Grant, now a major-general, struck first. In February 1862, he attacked and captured two key Confederate forts in Tennessee. Fort

Federal gunboats commanded by Andrew Foote bombard Fort Henry, Tennessee, as part of an assault coordinated by Union General Ulysses S. Grant in February 1862. Victories at Fort Henry on April 6, and at Fort Donelson 10 days later, secured control of Tennessee for the Union.

WORDS TO UNDERSTAND IN THIS CHAPTER

Killed, wounded, and *missing* is the full and descriptive way to describe what is often called by the shorter term ***casualties.***

Border states are those that sided with neither the Union nor the Confederacy. They maintained an uneasy kind of neutrality throughout the war.

Henry surrendered after only a day's fight, but Fort Donelson held on longer. And when Confederate General Simon Bolivar Buckner asked for honorable terms, he received the reply that made Grant famous: "No terms except an unconditional surrender can be accepted."

The following day, Buckner and 14,000 Confederates laid down their arms in the single largest surrender in the Civil War to date. Grant earned the nickname that stayed with him throughout the war. To millions in the North, he was "U.S. Grant," standing for "Unconditional Surrender Grant."

McClellan in the East

At the same time that Grant achieved spectacular success in the West, Union General George B. McClellan was whipping the Union's 110,000-man Army of the Potomac into shape. Born into a well-to-do Philadelphia

Major General George B. McClellan (1826–1881) became a national hero in 1862 for organizing and training the Army of the Potomac, the major Union army in the war's eastern theater. However, his caution on the battlefield frustrated President Lincoln.

family, McClellan was a splendid organizer. By April 1861, he had most of his men aboard steamers and sailboats heading down the Potomac River and then Chesapeake Bay. McClellan wanted to keep his troops from trudging through the countryside, and to bring them into position so they could speedily attack Richmond, the capital of the Confederacy.

President Lincoln recognized McClellan's brilliant tactical skill, but had doubts about his willingness to fight. Sometimes it seemed as if McClellan would do almost anything rather than engage his foe head-to-head.

The Battle of Shiloh

Fought on April 6, 1862, the Battle of Shiloh is named for the tiny white clapboard church that stood near the center of the battlefield. The Confederates, seeing what General Grant had done in the Western Theater, organized their forces, and pulled a big surprise. Their attack came on

On the first day of fighting at Shiloh, the Confederate forces seemed to have won a complete victory, capturing the Federal camps along with thousands of prisoners. However, the arrival of Union reinforcements late in the evening enabled Grant's army to counterattack the next day, driving the Confederates from the field.

the morning of April 6, and for a few hours, Grant's Union soldiers were in desperate shape.

The battle took place on the west side of the Tennessee River, and there were times when the Confederates nearly pushed the Union troops into the river itself. But at about 2 P.M. Confederate General Albert Sidney Johnston died from a bullet wound in his leg, and the heart went out of the Confederates. They continued to attack, but their pace slowed, and by early evening it was obvious that Grant's men would hold their position.

The cries of thousands of wounded men were heard all night long. Both sides had suffered roughly 8,000 *casualties*. Some Union troops believed Grant would stay on the defensive, or even withdraw, but he showed them what he was made of. On the following morning, April 7, 1862, Grant launched a series of counterattacks. The Confederates withdrew, and they knew they had lost their best chance in the Western Theater.

Shiloh was a turning point in the war. Until April 1862, men on both sides had fought skillfully and bravely, but without much anger or hatred toward the enemy. That changed after Shiloh. The bloodbath on the Tennessee River led many soldiers—Northerners and Southerners alike—to feel great anger toward their opponents.

Steamboats and Ironclad Ships

Steamboats had been around for nearly 40 years, but the idea of an ironclad boat or ship, one that could resist cannon blows, was relatively new. And when the Confederacy brought out the first ironclad warship—the C.S.S. *Virginia*—in the spring of 1862, it seemed that the South had a great new weapon.

 Sailing boats and ships had provided transportation on the water for centuries, but steam-powered boats and ships appeared only in the half-century before the Civil War.

The first naval battle involving warships covered in protective armor was fought off the coast of Virginia on March 9, 1862. The Union warship Monitor *is on the right in this painting of the battle; CSS* Virginia *is on the left. The battle ended in a draw, with neither ship able to inflict much damage on the other.*

The North, which had more factories than the South, rushed many of these boats into production, however. And when the U.S.S. *Monitor* fought the C.S.S. *Virginia* to a draw, near Hampton Roads, Virginia, it meant that the Union would keep its advantage at sea. At about the same time, the Union seized New Orleans. Steamboats proved a key factor in the Union strategy, and when the North took New Orleans, many Southerners began to lose heart. New Orleans, after all, was the largest and wealthiest city in the South.

One person who did not lose heart was Robert E. Lee.

The Seven Days' Battles

In June 1862, President Jefferson Davis named Robert E. Lee of Virginia, commander of the Army of Northern Virginia. The two men knew and liked each other. Even so, chances are that President Davis did not realize just how important this appointment was.

General Robert E. Lee (1807–1870), commander of the Army of Northern Virginia, was among the most respected military leaders of the Civil War.

Born near Alexandria, Virginia, in 1807, Lee was the son of Light Horse Harry Lee, a prominent cavalry commander in the American Revolution. Lee was now in his mid-50s, but he had the spirit and energy of a younger man. And when Union General McClellan brought the Army of the Potomac close to the all-important city of Richmond, Lee chose to strike, even though he was outnumbered.

The Seven Days' Battles, at the end of June 1862, turned into a terrible bloodbath. Some 20,000 Confederates were killed, wounded, or missing when the weeklong conflict ended. But Lee had guessed correctly. General McClellan did not have the stomach for a prolonged fight. He withdrew his men, by water, to the area around Washington, D.C.

The Second Battle of Bull Run/Manassas

Robert E. Lee knew how outnumbered he was, and how many advantages the North had over the South. He believed, however, that one major Confederate victory, won on Northern soil, would discourage the people up North. Then, too, he continued to hope that England or France would forge an alliance with the Confederacy. Lee, therefore, asked President Davis for permission to invade the North.

President Davis was aware of the risks. He agreed just the same. He and Lee were different in many ways, but they were both risk-takers.

In August 1862, Lee defeated the Army of the Potomac on almost the same battlefield where the First Battle of Bull Run/Manassas had been fought. This victory encouraged Lee to be even bolder, and in September 1862, he and 70,000 men crossed the Potomac River, entering Maryland.

The Cigar-Box Tissue

On September 10, 1862, Union General George B. McClellan received a gift that seemed to have been heaven-sent. Two of his soldiers brought him a set of Robert E. Lee's specific commands, wrapped in cigar-box tissue.

Opening the orders, McClellan saw at once that Lee had divided the Army of Northern Virginia, sending part of it north, part of it west, and a third part to attack the federal armory at Harpers Ferry. The Army of the Potomac already outnumbered the Confederates. Possessing these orders meant McClellan could concentrate his forces and destroy the sections of Lee's army one by one.

He did not do so. McClellan moved with appalling slowness. Although Lee was in a dangerous position, he managed to gather 40,000 troops and establish a defensive position at Sharpsburg, Maryland along Antietam Creek.

The Battle of Antietam

On the morning of September 17, 1862, McClellan and the Army of the Potomac finally began a massive assault on the Confederates, in and around the little town of Sharpsburg, Maryland. Though they did not know it, the 120,000 men on both sides, combined, were engaged in the largest battle ever fought in North America.

All day long the Union pushed and pressed, and there were several moments when the entire Confederate defense buckled and was about to collapse. On each occasion, the Confederates were rescued, either by the arrival of reinforcements or by General McClellan's timidity. Even in the late afternoon, one big push could have succeeded, but McClellan held back. As a result, Lee and the Army of Northern Virginia survived.

The losses were terrible, however. Each side suffered about 11,000 casualties that day. Antietam was the bloodiest single day of the Civil War, and it also marked the high-water mark of Confederate success. Through luck, skill, and sheer daring, Lee had invaded the North and come close to victory. Instead, however, he had to retreat across the Potomac, and back into northern Virginia.

McClellan, amazingly, allowed Lee and the Confederates to escape. The person who was most upset by this was President Lincoln. Unlike McClellan, and quite a few other Union generals, Lincoln had the killer instinct. He knew better than to allow a dangerous opponent to escape to fight another day.

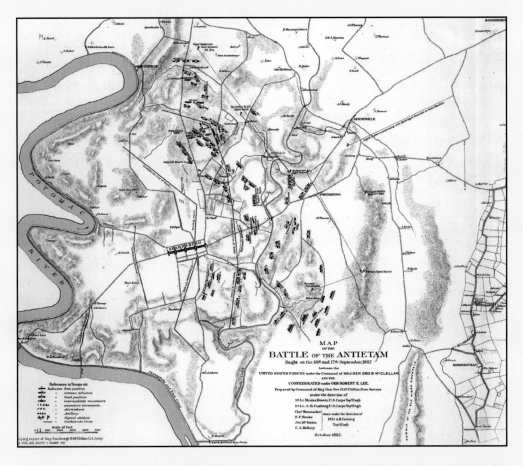

This map shows the distribution of Union (blue) attackers and Confederate (red) defenders around the town of Sharpsburg, Maryland. More than 1,500 Confederate soldiers lost their lives in the September 1862 clash that today is called the Battle of Antietam, with over 7,700 wounded and 1,000 captured. Casualties were even higher on the Union side, with over 2,100 killed, 9,500 wounded, and 750 missing. However, the Army of Northern Virginia retreated from the battlefield, allowing General McClellan to claim Antietam as a Union victory.

WOMEN IN THE WAR

Today we take for granted that women can, if they choose, participate in war to some degree. This was not the case in the Civil War.

Very few women served in combat, and those who did concealed their gender. On the other hand, many women provided assistance to the men engaged in battle. For instance, Clara Barton, born in Massachusetts in 1820, was the most prominent female nurse during the war, but there were countless others as well.

Freedom for Most

On September 23, 1862, five days after the Battle of Antietam, President Lincoln issued the broadest, most far-reaching proclamation ever handed down by a president. Though the Emancipation Proclamation was long, wordy, and did not free all the slaves, perhaps 80 percent of them were covered by this document. Lincoln declared that all persons held in slavery in areas currently in rebellion against the Union would, on the first of January 1863, be forever free.

Lincoln's critics, then and today, have pointed out that he did not free the slaves who lived in the so-called *border states* of Maryland, Delaware, Kentucky, and Missouri. Lincoln doubted whether he had the authority to do so. Just as important, he did not wish to drive the border states into the arms of the Confederacy. Even the sharpest of Lincoln's critics admitted, however, that he had taken a huge step forward.

The Battle of Fredericksburg

President Lincoln was not satisfied with the half-success at Antietam. Far from it. In November 1862, he finally fired General McClellan, replacing him with General Ambrose Burnside.

Burnside was a faithful corps commander, someone who had been with the Army of the Potomac through thick and thin. He was also famous for his sideburns, and the modern word sideburns comes from a corruption of his last name.

Prompted by President Lincoln, Burnside moved the Army of the Potomac into action in December 1862. Bringing pontoon bridges with them, the Union soldiers marched across the half-frozen countryside of northern Virginia and crossed the Rapidan River at the little town of Fredericksburg. What neither Burnside nor his men realized was the extent to which the Army of Northern Virginia had prepared for their arrival.

Robert E. Lee and Stonewall Jackson, who were the top Confederate generals, had fortified a series of hills on the southern side of the Rapidan. Lee could hardly believe that Burnside would be so obliging as to make a frontal attack, but that is just what the Union forces did. On December 17, 1862, the Army of the Potomac made one hopeless attack after another, suffering 11,000 casualties.

Burnside withdrew to Washington, D.C. The major fighting of 1862 was over.

TEXT-DEPENDENT QUESTIONS

1. Where do we get the modern term *sideburns*?
2. What was the single bloodiest battle of 1862?

RESEARCH PROJECT

Find a map of the state of Virginia, photocopy it, and then mark in red the places where the big battles of 1861 and 1862 were fought.

Chapter 3

YEAR OF DECISION

At the beginning of 1863, it seemed like the war would drag on for a long time. The Union Army seemed to be gaining the advantage in the Western Theater, with several notable victories. Despite their strategic victory at Antietam, however, Union forces had struggled to defeat the Confederate army in battle. Meanwhile, General Lee was preparing an offensive strike into Union territory.

The 20th Maine Infantry Regiment's staunch defense of Little Round Top prevented the Confederate Army from gaining control of the high ground, and helped lead to a Union victory at Gettysburg. That battle in July 1863 is considered a turning point of the Civil War.

WORDS TO UNDERSTAND IN THIS CHAPTER

To *amputate* a limb means to cut it off, because it has been too badly damaged to heal properly.

A *siege* occurs when military forces surround an enemy town or fortification, cutting off essential supplies, with the aim of compelling the defenders to surrender.

Grant and the West

At the beginning of 1863, General Grant had his sights firmly fixed on Vicksburg, the last Confederate city on either side of the Mississippi. Located on the eastern side, in the state of Mississippi, Vicksburg had strong natural defenses, backed up by excellent human-made ones. The Yazoo Delta protected the city on its northern and eastern flanks, and fire from the city's many cannons endangered any attacking vessel. Grant's largest problem was how to conquer Vicksburg.

During the winter of 1863, Grant tried several maneuvers, all of which failed. But in February, a squadron of Union steamboats managed to get past the Confederate gun batteries with little damage. This encouraged Grant to try something bold. In March 1863, he brought 40,000 men to the western side of the Mississippi, and marched them through areas in which there were no roads. Then in April, he re-crossed the Mississippi, a large distance south of Vicksburg. Suddenly, Grant and his troops were on solid ground with good roads.

While Grant and his soldiers battled against two Confederate Armies, the attention of millions of Americans—North and South—shifted to the Eastern Theater.

The Battle of Chancellorsville

Early in May 1863, Union General Joseph Hooker led 110,000 soldiers of the Army of the Potomac out of their camps near Washington, D.C.

After crossing the Rapidan River, Hooker and his troops entered an area known as the Wilderness. One of the few homes in the area belonged to a man named Chancellor, whose name was given to the battle that followed.

Hooker was a first-rate leader of men. He was no George B. McClellan. At Chancellorsville, however, Hooker let down first himself and then his troops. Though he had 110,000 soldiers to Lee's 70,000, Hooker did not push aggressively, and this allowed Lee to launch a masterful counterstrike.

Knowing that the outcome might determine the life or death of the Confederacy, Lee chose to divide his already

Major General Joseph Hooker (1814–1879) gained the nickname "Fighting Joe" for his aggressive style as a corps commander during McClellan's 1862 campaign in Virginia. However, Hooker was unexpectedly indecisive on the eve of battle with the Confederate Army in May 1863, and it resulted in a humbling defeat for the Army of the Potomac at Chancellorsville.

outnumbered force. He kept 30,000 troops close at hand, 10,000 in reserve, and sent 30,000 others, led by Stonewall Jackson, to make a dramatic, all-day march around the Union's right flank. If Hooker and the Federals learned about this maneuver, they could have destroyed either section. But Hooker remained quiet all day on May 5, 1863, and Stonewall Jackson's attack, on his right, caught him completely off guard.

A major rout took place, with the Confederates capturing thousands of Union troops. Only the arrival of dusk prevented a major catastrophe for the North. Stonewall Jackson felt confident about what he had accomplished, and he planned to follow up on the Confederate victory the next day. That was when disaster struck.

Riding back from a look at the Union lines, Jackson was shot and wounded by his own troops. In the darkness, they thought he was a Union cavalryman.

Jackson was wounded in three places, but the wound to his left arm was the worst. The arm was *amputated*, but this did not save his life. Jackson died on May 10, 1863.

Robert E. Lee commented that Jackson had lost his left arm, but that he had lost his right. It was a fair statement, given that Jackson was the ideal subordinate, the number-two man who could carry out the ambitious plans of the commanding general.

Chancellorsville was a great Confederate triumph. Lee lost about 11,000 troops, but he inflicted 16,000 casualties on Hooker, and drove him from the battlefield. But the death of Stonewall Jackson cast a pall over the victory. Meanwhile, things in the Western Theater were going from bad to worse for the South.

The Siege of Vicksburg

Ulysses S. Grant seized the advantage, and momentum, in the West. Having re-crossed, to the eastern side of the Mississippi River, he outmaneuvered two Confederate commanders. General Joseph E. Johnston had to give up control of Jackson, the capital of Mississippi, and General John Pemberton was thoroughly beaten at the Battle of Champion Hill. After this loss, Pemberton had no choice but to fall back to the defenses around Vicksburg. Grant, who at moments like these acted like a tiger, pushed quickly right up to the city walls.

Grant's first direct assault was a failure, and he reluctantly settled down to impose a *siege* on the city. The outcome was not in doubt, however, because he had Vicksburg surrounded on three sides, and the Union Navy choked off supplies from the Mississippi River. But the siege was long and costly for both sides.

Invasion of the North

The death of Stonewall Jackson was a bitter blow to the Southern cause, but the Battle of Chancellorsville was Lee's greatest victory. In tactical terms, he routed his foe, and inflicted 16,000 casualties. The 11,000 Confederate casualties were more than the South could afford, however.

Lee knew this quite well. He was certain that a Confederate victory on Northern soil was the only way to turn the tide in the South's favor. So he asked Confederate President Jefferson Davis for permission to march into Maryland. This was granted, and on June 21, 1863, Lee and about 70,000 Confederates crossed the Potomac.

General Ulysses S. Grant (1822–1885) besieged the city of Vicksburg, Mississippi in July 1863. Grant recognized that capturing the city would prevent Confederate ships from using the Mississippi River to transport soldiers and supplies.

Unlike the brief invasion of the previous year, the Confederates made excellent time. Some of their cavalry units were soon in Pennsylvania, and the bulk of the Army of Northern Virginia was not far behind. The only trouble was that the Confederates had no supply wagons. They lived off the countryside, seizing Maryland potatoes, Pennsylvania corn, and other foodstuffs.

President Lincoln could hardly believe the Confederate success. He fired General Hooker, replacing him with General George B. Meade. Meade was from Pennsylvania, and he was a cautious, thoughtful general. Even so, the huge confrontation with the Confederates at Gettysburg came not as a result of anyone's plan, but because of the Confederate need for shoes.

On the afternoon of June 30, 1863, a Confederate regiment approached the little town of Gettysburg, Pennsylvania, which had a shoe factory. Union forces had been tracking the movement of the Confederates as they marched north, and had established a foothold in southern Pennsylvania to defend against a Confederate invasion. The Confederates withdrew on June 30, planning to return the next day. As luck, or irony, would have it, the great Battle of Gettysburg was fought in reverse, with the Confederate forces coming from the north, and the Union forces approaching from the south.

The Battle of Gettysburg

About 2,400 people lived in Gettysburg, which has a long row of hills and ridges to its south and east. Who gained, and held, the high ground would likely win the battle.

The Battle of Gettysburg began at around 9 A.M. on July 1, 1863. A Confederate brigade ran into two regiments of Union cavalry. Throughout this first day, Confederates arrived in greater numbers than Federals. And when Robert E. Lee arrived, at about 2 P.M., he saw an opportunity for a major victory. His men pressed all afternoon, and when darkness came they had gained control of the town, the shoe factory, and much of the lowland. They had not taken the heights, however.

On the morning of July 2, 1863, Lee conferred with his generals. At times like this he sorely missed the presence of Stonewall Jackson. Lee's generals believed he should abandon the town of Gettysburg, withdraw to different terrain, and fight again another day. This made excellent sense, but Lee was in a fighting mood. The enemy was there, on the ridge, and he wanted to strike.

The second day of the Battle of Gettysburg—July 2, 1863—was far bloodier than the first. All day long, the Confederates attacked the hills and ridges on the western side of the Union position, and there were times when they almost broke through. Each "almost" cost the Confederates

This Confederate sharpshooter was killed on the second day of the Battle of Gettysburg, in the rocky area known as "Devil's Den."

far too many men, however, and when the sun went down it was evident that both sides had taken a severe beating.

On the morning of the third day—July 3, 1863—Lee surprised his generals by saying one more attack would be made. The Confederates had pressed the Yankees hard on the previous day, and one final assault, made straight up the middle, would ensure victory, according to Lee. The other generals, including James Longstreet, were pessimistic, but Lee rejected their concerns. The attack would be made in midafternoon, he declared.

At noon, the Confederate artillery began an immense rain of cannon and mortar fire against the 5,000 Union defenders at the middle section of the Northern defenses. Thousands of cannon shots exploded on the horizon, but Lee and his men could not see how much damage was being done. Then, almost precisely at 4 P.M., General George Pickett led 15,000 fresh Confederate troops from their shelter in the woods to the open field that inclined toward the Union defenses. Drums were beat, trumpets sounded, and the long, elegant wave of Confederates began an orderly march toward their foe.

For several minutes the Confederates moved unimpeded, but then came terrible blasts of fire from muskets, rifles, and cannon. The noise was deafening, and the casualties were appalling. But the Confederates—men of the Army of Northern Virginia who had achieved so many victories— kept right on marching.

About two-thirds of the way up the hill, the Confederates encountered a split-rail fence. This slowed them down, as the troops either had to climb over the fence or crawl beneath it. When they came on the other side of that fence, the Union rifle and musket fire became ever more deadly. About 400 Confederates, through sheer willpower, did manage to reach the top of the hill, but they were quickly killed or captured. The others finally turned and ran back the way they had come.

Seven thousand Confederates were killed, wounded, or missing that day. Pickett's Charge was the worst loss the South suffered in the entire war.

Amazingly, Union General George Meade did not press his advantage. Lee and the Army of Northern Virginia escaped south, bloodied but still intact.

Surrender at Vicksburg

While General Meade and the Army of the Potomac defeated Lee and the Army of Northern Virginia at Gettysburg, Generals Grant and William T. Sherman pressed the Confederate defenders at Vicksburg hard. The artillery bombardments were constant. And on the afternoon of July 3, 1863—the same afternoon as Pickett's Charge—Confederate General John Pemberton asked for terms of surrender.

Pemberton received the painful answer that Confederate generals were accustomed to: nothing but an immediate and unconditional surrender.

On July 4, 1863, the Confederates yielded Vicksburg, and laid down their arms. Now there was no Confederate fortress on the Mississippi River, nothing to prevent the Union from pressing its huge advantage in the Western Theater. And the person who, justly, received most of the praise for that victory was Ulysses S. Grant.

More Battles Out West and the Gettysburg Address

By the fall of 1863, things were going very badly for the Confederates, and nowhere was this more evident than in southeastern Tennessee. The

After the disastrous defeat at Chancellorsville, General Joe Hooker was transferred to the Western Theater. There, he restored his reputation with a successful assault on a strong Confederate position at Lookout Mountain, Georgia, on November 24, 1863. Hooker's men then helped General George Thomas's troops to clear Missionary Ridge of Confederate soldiers the next day. These victories ended a Confederate threat to Chattanooga, Tennessee, and opened the way for Union troops to invade the deep South.

Confederates managed to claim a victory at the Battle of Chickamauga, but they failed to capture the railroad hub of Chattanooga. General Braxton Bragg and his 40,000 Confederate troops occupied Lookout Mountain, directly overlooking Chattanooga, but their failure to make a quick strike allowed the Union to bring in reinforcements. In November 1863, Ulysses S. Grant, who had been summoned to rescue the situation, struck at the Confederates.

The Union charge that resulted in the capture of Lookout Mountain was electrifying. Troops of the Army of the Cumberland charged across hundreds of yards of open field to seize the Confederate rifle pits at the bottom of the mountain. The Confederates, several hundred feet above, pelted them with rifle fire.

No one gave the order. No one planned it. Suddenly, thousands of men from the Army of the Cumberland simply rose out of the rifle pits and began running and climbing. The Confederates should have stopped them with artillery fire, but their cannon muzzles jammed. The Union forces should have encountered too much opposition: natural and human-made. But they did not. Twenty minutes later, Union soldiers were on top of the mountain, and General Bragg's Confederates were in full retreat. If Gettysburg revealed the power of the Union on the defense, the fighting around Chattanooga showed that Northern soldiers could win when attacking their foes, and do so in grand style.

Days later, President Lincoln arrived at Gettysburg, to dedicate the new national cemetery for those who had died on that battlefield. Lincoln wrote the Gettysburg Address while on his train ride to Gettysburg. His words, given in a speech that lasted less than three minutes, have never

Lincoln wrote the Gettysburg Address on the back of an envelope as he traveled by train from Washington to Gettysburg.

been forgotten: "We here highly resolve that these dead shall not have died in vain—that this nation . . . shall have a new birth of freedom—and that government of the people, by the people, for the people, shall not perish from the earth."

TEXT-DEPENDENT QUESTIONS

1. How great a risk did Robert E. Lee take when he divided his army at the opening stage of the Battle of Chancellorsville?

2. At which battle did Lee become stubborn, meaning that he did not listen to good advice?

3. How important was the split-rail fence at the Battle of Gettysburg?

RESEARCH PROJECT

Take the number of Confederates killed at Pickett's Charge and divide it into the total white population of the Confederacy (see below). Then, write a paragraph explaining how important, or unimportant, Pickett's Charge was for the Confederacy.

- 8,000,000 whites in Southern states, as of census of 1860
- 7,000 white Southern soldiers killed or wounded during Pickett's Charge

Chapter 4

YEAR OF BLOOD

By the beginning of 1864, most people—on both sides—believed that the North would eventually win the war. Not only did the Union have more men, more equipment, and more factories, but it had now developed some outstanding generals. But the South had great generals of its own, including Robert E. Lee, and there was lots of fight left among Confederate troops, even though the soldiers of the Army of Northern Virginia knew they faced almost overwhelming odds against them.

African-American soldiers attack Fort Wagner, a Confederate stronghold on Morris Island, South Carolina. During the Civil War more than 180,000 blacks—most of them freed slaves— served in the Union army and navy.

Grant and Sherman

In March 1864, Grant arrived in Washington, D.C. for the first time. He stayed at Willard's Hotel, the most *fashionable* place in town, but he did not look fashionable, or even pre-sentable. He dressed and acted much as he always had, with more sloppiness than dash. He also smoked cigars constantly. Most Northerners agreed that these things did not matter. Grant was the victor from the Western Theater, now on hand to gain victory in the East. He was the man of the hour.

When Grant was promoted to commander of all Union armies, his trusted subordinate General William T. Sherman (1820–1891) took command of the armies in the Western Theater.

President Lincoln agreed. He told Grant he did not need to know the specifics of his plans, only that he wanted Grant to pursue the enemy with 100 percent of his power. Lincoln knew he had finally found a general with great fighting spirit.

 ## WORDS TO UNDERSTAND IN THIS CHAPTER

Someone who is *fashionable* is stylish or conforms to the latest trends or styles in dress or behavior.

Not to swap horses in midstream used to be a regular expression in American life. It means that one should stay the course, and not make any radical changes while in the middle of a dangerous situation.

In the weeks before he moved against Robert E. Lee, Grant conferred with General William Tecumseh Sherman. The two were good friends, as well as military colleagues, and when people later asked Sherman what their conversation was like, he replied, "He was to go for Lee, and I was to go for Johnston." In other words, Grant and Sherman intended to destroy the remaining Confederate Armies, rather than worry about territory, land, or even cities and towns.

Grant in the East

In May 1864, Grant led the Army of the Potomac over the Rapidan River. In almost precisely the same place as the Battle of Chancellorsville a year

The bodies of dead Confederate soldiers are lined up for burial on the battlefield at Spotsylvania. Lee's army absorbed 5,000 fewer casualties than the Federals during the two-week Battle of the Wilderness. But with a nonslave population that was roughly one-quarter the population of the Union states, the Confederacy couldn't easily replace its losses, whereas the Union could. Recognizing this, Grant was prepared to wage a war of attrition, taking high casualties if necessary to grind down the Confederate army.

earlier, Grant battled Lee. The Battle of the Wilderness, as it is called, was especially bloody and brutal. Each side suffered more than 10,000 casualties.

Many of Grant's foot soldiers feared that he, like other Union generals before him, would lose heart and quit. But Grant took just the opposite tack. The day after the Battle of the Wilderness ended, Grant had his troops march west, and then south, moving to outflank Lee. The Confederates countered, and the two sides fought another bloody battle at Spotsylvania Court House in Virginia. Grant moved west and then south yet again, and Lee had to counter. An even bloodier and uglier battle was fought at Cold Harbor, Virginia. Eight thousand Union soldiers were killed or wounded in two hours' time.

People in the North labeled Grant "the Butcher," and called for his resignation. Others urged President Lincoln to fire Grant. But Lincoln remained firm. Grant was a fighting general, he said, and all such men are expected to have casualties in their ranks. Lincoln kept Grant as general-in-chief of all the Union Armies. Grant repaid Lincoln by outflanking Lee, crossing the James River, and nearly capturing Richmond, Virginia.

Grant came within a day or two of victory. However, just enough Confederates reinforced Richmond and the railroad town of Petersburg to keep him from claiming victory. As a result, Grant and Lee were soon locked in a life-or-death siege that encompassed Richmond, Petersburg, and the 20 miles (32km) that lay in between. The chances of a Union victory were excellent, but the siege took longer than anyone expected.

 Ulysses S. Grant hoped and expected that the explosion of the Crater on July 30, 1864 would allow him to defeat Lee and win the war, perhaps on that very day.

Sherman in the West

In May 1864, Sherman moved south from Chattanooga with about 110,000 troops. Most were veterans of many battles, and their equipment was far superior to the Confederates'. Even so, Confederate General Joseph Johnston—who had been at the First Battle of Bull Run/Manassas in 1861—maneuvered so well that the campaign resembled a dance, with the Confederates and the Union forces flanking and then outflanking each other. Few battles, or even skirmishes, were fought until the Confederates had to defend Atlanta. The city had only about 10,000 inhabitants, but it was the railroad junction for practically all

This painting shows Union and Confederate troops fighting for Atlanta in 1864. The capture of Georgia's largest city by the Union army was a major blow to the Confederacy.

that remained of the Confederacy. If Atlanta fell, transportation in the Confederacy would grind to a halt, and the various Southern regiments would be unable to coordinate their movements or even communicate with each other.

Sherman's first major attack was at Kennesaw Mountain, 20 miles (32 km) northwest of Atlanta. His troops suffered over 2,000 casualties, and were repelled by the Southern forces. Sherman went back to maneuvering, and by late August he had almost encircled the all-important Southern city. Joseph Johnston was replaced by General John B. Hood, who evacuated his troops from Atlanta on September 1, 1864, ceding the city to the North.

Lincoln's Reelection

In the summer of 1864, it was by no means certain that Abraham Lincoln would win a second term in the White House. His opponent was George B. McClellan, the former commander of the Army of the Potomac. Lincoln ran as the Republican candidate, and McClellan ran as the Democratic nominee. Lincoln was nervous, even depressed, but the news of Atlanta's fall brought him back to life. The voters reacted the same way.

Encouraged by the fall of Atlanta, Northern voters decided *not to* "*swap horses in midstream.*" Lincoln won by a substantial margin in the popular vote, and by a large majority in the electoral vote. Lincoln's reelection was a major boost for Northern morale, and it led to depressed spirits in the South. Very little chance of any kind of Southern victory now remained.

Black Soldiers

The Emancipation Proclamation had formally liberated almost 4 million African-Americans, many of whom were eager to fight for the Union. The first two all-black regiments were recruited in Massachusetts, but it was decided that they must have white men as officers. This, and a lower pay rate, angered many African-Americans, but they knew their future depended on swift, strong action.

The Massachusetts 54th, gallantly led by Lieutenant-Colonel Robert Gould Shaw, fought courageously at the Battle of Fort Wagner, just outside Charleston, in July 1863. Most whites who observed the battle drew the same conclusion: these black men fought just as well and just as hard as anyone else. The need to prove themselves often led African-Americans to take greater risks and endure larger sacrifices. Recruitment picked up in most states of the Union, and when the war ended there were about 200,000 black men under arms.

Union warships commanded by David Farragut pass Fort Morgan, part of the Confederate defense at Mobile Bay, Alabama. Although one Union monitor struck a Confederate underwater mine (called a torpedo) and quickly sank, Farragut ordered the rest of his fleet to continue the assault, resulting in an important Union victory. The capture of Mobile Bay in August 1864 closed one of the few remaining Confederate ports, making it harder for the Confederacy to receive much-needed supplies and munitions.

The Crater and the Valley

On July 30, 1864, the Confederate defensive lines at Petersburg, Virginia were shaken by an enormous explosion. Union engineers had tunneled far underground, set explosives, and the results were spectacular. The explosion created an enormous crater.

Up to that point, almost everything was going right from the Union point of view. But ten minutes later, everything began to go wrong. The crater had a sharp upward curve, meaning that oncoming Union regiments were fired at by Confederates, who saw them as sitting ducks. Attacks at other places along the line failed to ease the pressure, and at the end of the day the North suffered almost 3,000 casualties. This was an embarrassing defeat.

It was another matter in the Valley, however.

The Shenandoah Valley, in the western part of Virginia, is one of the most magnificent areas of natural beauty in the nation. Throughout the war, towns and farms in the Valley changed hands, with first the Confederates and then Union troops winning control. In the fall of 1864, the Union made a powerful effort to change this seesaw state of affairs. General Philip Sheridan led a large army, almost equally composed of infantry and cavalry, into the Valley. He won a major victory in November, and from then on, the Valley was in Union hands.

The First Thanksgiving

In the last months of 1864, President Lincoln considered a request for a formal day of thanksgiving. This was not a new concept in America. The Pilgrims and the Puritans had selected many days for the giving of thanks. But for the nation as a whole to do so was something quite novel. Secretary of War Edwin M. Stanton approved the measure, and on the last Thursday in November 1864, people throughout the North celebrated Thanksgiving for the first time.

In the Southern states, there was little to be thankful for. Besides tremendous losses in manpower, the people of the Confederacy faced crippling inflation. The prices of some goods had increased by three- or even fourfold. The diaries of prominent Southern families show that even they went through a hard winter and a miserable Christmas, because it was so difficult to procure even the most basic items.

TEXT-DEPENDENT QUESTIONS

1. Where did Grant, and most other leading Union military officers, stay when he was in Washington, D.C.?

2. The fall of which Confederate city propelled Lincoln to win the election of 1864?

3. Americans have been holding days of fast and thanksgiving for centuries. When did they first celebrate a general thanksgiving throughout the land?

RESEARCH PROJECT

More than 180,000 African Americans served with the Union military during the Civil War. After the war ended, some of these men continued to serve in U.S. Army regiments in the West. Using your school library or the Internet, find out more about the "Buffalo Soldiers," as the men of the segregated Ninth and Tenth U.S. Cavalry Regiments were known. Write a one-page report on their activities and experiences, and present it to your class.

Chapter 5

MARTYRDOM AND NATIONHOOD

When the war began, many people—in the North and the South alike—looked on Abraham Lincoln as a lightweight, someone who had not been tested. By the beginning of 1865, that view had changed radically. Many people—whether they loved or hated him— regarded Lincoln as a great and powerful leader.

Jefferson Davis, by contrast, had never developed into a truly national leader. That was not entirely his fault. The Confederacy was built as a

A Union Army artillery battery prepares for battle in Georgia. Sherman's March to the Sea, which culminated in the capture of the Confederate port of Savannah, showed that the Confederacy could no longer defend itself.

WORDS TO UNDERSTAND IN THIS CHAPTER

A *martyr* is a person who gives his life for a cause. Martyrdom is the act itself.

The idea of *total war* has been around for thousands of years, but the expression comes to us from Grant and Sherman, who believed in using all means necessary to defeat the South.

compact between the Southern states, not as a genuine nation. The lack of strong leadership cost the South dearly.

Sherman's March to the Sea

In November 1864, Sherman and 60,000 troops left Atlanta. They headed east toward the coast in groups, rather than as a single, compact body. As a result, they caused greater destruction.

Many Southerners, Georgians especially, complained that Sherman violated the rules of combat by making war on civilians. Many small farmers had their harvest, their very livelihood, seized by advancing Union soldiers.

Sherman knew this would happen. He viewed the destruction, of buildings and railroad lines especially, as a necessary tactic. The North had to wage *total war* in order to break the South's will to resist, he declared.

By Christmas Day 1864, Sherman was in Savannah, and at the beginning of 1865 he was marching north through South Carolina. The chances that he would link up with Ulysses S. Grant were good. The Confederate Army was no longer strong enough to prevent them from going wherever they wanted.

An Attempt at Peace

In January 1865, when things looked very dark, the Confederacy sent a delegation of four men to seek peace terms with the North. One of the four was Alexander H. Stephens, the vice-president of the Confederacy.

President Lincoln did not allow the men into Washington, D.C. To do so would have provoked anger among the Republican majority in the House of Representatives. When Grant met with the peacemakers, however, he found they did not have the authority to agree to a complete surrender. From Grant's point of view, and Lincoln's, too, that meant the negotiations were not legitimate. The Confederate peacemakers went home, having accomplished nothing.

The Final Campaign

Throughout March of 1865, Grant's Army of the Potomac probed the Confederate defenses of Richmond and Petersburg. Everywhere the Northern soldiers looked, they found weakness.

Union soldiers overrun a Confederate battery at Petersburg, April 2, 1865. The fall of the Confederate defenses at Petersburg enabled the Union Army to capture Richmond, the Confederate capital.

During the Civil War, many Southern cities were devastated as the Union attempted end the rebellion. This is an April 1865 view of damaged buildings in Charleston, South Carolina—the city where the first shots of the war had been fired four years earlier.

Lee and the Army of Northern Virginia launched one last offensive. At the Battle of Fort Stedman, Lee attacked and made some initial gains, but his troops were soon thrown back with great losses. Lee knew he was defeated, and on the morning of April 1, 1865, he and his troops evacuated Richmond. Lee headed west.

Confederate President Jefferson Davis learned about the evacuation of the troops just in time. He and the members of his Cabinet were soon on their way out of the city as well, traveling by train.

Ulysses S. Grant wished, of course, to savor his triumph, but there was no time. He and the Army of the Potomac were soon in full pursuit of Lee and the Army of Northern Virginia. It fell, therefore, to President Lincoln to make the triumphal entry to Richmond, where he arrived on April 9, 1865.

Lincoln came, escorted only by a few dozen Navy sailors, armed with carbines. He and his escort were appalled by the devastation they encountered. Richmond looked as if it had been hit by one enormous bombshell that had exploded into dozens of fragments.

Lincoln walked the streets. He was hailed by African Americans. Some of them dropped at his feet and called him Father Abraham. He asked them to rise, and said a person should only kneel to God. In some ways, this was Lincoln's finest moment. He did not gloat over his victory, and his heart was moved with compassion for the Confederates, who had fallen to such a lowly state.

Lincoln returned to Washington, D.C., where victory celebrations were planned.

Surrender at Appomattox

Lee and the Army of Northern Virginia fled from Richmond, but they were pursued across the countryside by Grant and the Army of the Potomac. After one last battle, at Sayler's Creek, Virginia, Lee knew his cause was hopeless. He sent a letter to Grant, proposing that they meet to discuss surrender terms.

On the afternoon of Sunday, April 8, 1865, Lee arrived at the home of Wilmer McLean, in the tiny village of Appomattox Court House. Grant

General Grant watches General Lee sign the terms of surrender at Appomattox Court House, April 9, 1865.

and his staff arrived half an hour later, and after some cordial greetings, Lee and Grant began to work out the terms of surrender.

With other defeated Confederate generals, Grant had been dismissive, even rude. He had never offered terms, and simply demanded unconditional surrender. The meeting with Lee was different. Grant knew that Lee was greatly admired in the South, and that even some in the North quietly admired his bravery. It would not do, therefore, to demand anything. Lee must be seen as having yielded willingly.

The two men talked for more than an hour, during which they agreed that all of Lee's forces would lay down their arms. It was further agreed that they would be allowed to take their horses and mules, and that the Confederate officers would be allowed to keep their sidearms. Taken aback by Grant's generosity, Lee declared that these terms would have a good impact on his men.

When they parted, late that afternoon, Lee and Grant rode back to their respective camps. The surrender ceremony took place the following day, April 9, 1865. Lee traveled back to his home in Richmond, and Grant headed to Washington, D.C., to take part in the victory celebrations.

In the western theater, Confederate General Joseph Johnston still had an army in the field, and he did not surrender until April 26, 1865. Even so, almost everyone understood that Lee's surrender meant the end of the war. More than Jefferson Davis—who was captured that same April—Lee was the heart and soul of the Confederacy. When he yielded, most other Confederates did the same.

Lincoln's Death

On Friday, April 14, 1865, Lincoln met with his Cabinet (General Grant was also present). When members of the Cabinet asked how Southerners should be treated, Lincoln said, "Let 'em up easy." This was his traditional attitude toward a conquered foe, an attitude Lincoln had learned during his backwoods days in Illinois.

As Cabinet business wound down, Lincoln asked if anyone would like to accompany him and his wife, First Lady Mary Todd Lincoln, to Ford's Theatre. General Grant declined, because he and his wife were heading to Philadelphia that evening. Captain Henry Rathbone and his fiancée, Clara H. Harris, agreed to accompany the Lincolns.

At 7 P.M. the Lincolns and their guests arrived at Ford's Theatre, in downtown Washington, D.C. Going to the theater was one of President Lincoln's fondest distractions, and he and his wife had attended plays there many times before. But this night would change the history of the nation.

John Wilkes Booth was a handsome young man with a daredevil personality. Raised in Maryland in a family of actors, Booth was a Confederate sympathizer who detested Lincoln and the possibility that African-Americans would one day become full citizens with full rights, including the right to vote. Booth had decided to assassinate the president a few days earlier. He planned the attack with a small group Confederate sympathizers, who were plotting to kill other high-ranking members of the U.S. government at the same time.

On the evening of April 14, Booth snuck into the back section of Ford's Theatre, went up the stairs, and burst into the president's box. Booth shot Lincoln in the back of the head. Captain Rathbone rose, and Booth slashed his arm with a knife. Jumping the 10 feet (3m) down to the stage, Booth cried out, "Thus ever to tyrants!" and disappeared.

Lincoln's Martyrdom

Lincoln lived until 7 A.M. on Saturday, April 15, 1865. He died surrounded by members of his Cabinet.

 Lincoln was the second president to die in office. The first was William Henry Harrison, who died of natural causes soon after his inauguration.

The news spread rapidly because of the telegraph, and people all over the North went into mourning. Some Confederates cheered, but most of them either had a grudging respect for Lincoln or suspected that his death meant bad news for them.

After funeral services in Washington, Lincoln's body was taken by train to his home in Illinois, by way of Philadelphia, New York, Buffalo, and other major cities. Some 3 million people saw the funeral train as it passed.

By the time his body was laid to rest, Lincoln had become not merely a hero but also a ***martyr***, meaning someone who gives his life for a cause. To be sure, hundreds of thousands of soldiers had already done that very thing. But through Lincoln's death, all the other Union war dead became martyrs as well—martyrs in the cause of nationalism.

Jefferson Davis, by contrast, was seen as a traitor. He spent two years in a federal penitentiary before being released. He died of lung disease in 1889.

Robert E. Lee died well before Jefferson Davis. He died of heart disease in 1870.

Ulysses S. Grant died of throat cancer in 1885. Shortly before his death, Grant wrote his military memoirs. Published by American author and humorist Mark Twain, these are believed to be among the best-written of all military memoirs.

William Tecumseh Sherman lived the longest of the major figures of the Civil War. He died in 1893. By then, most people could see that the Civil War had altered the history of war, and changed the fate of the nation.

The Civil War was the most destructive conflict of its time. Some 750,000 people

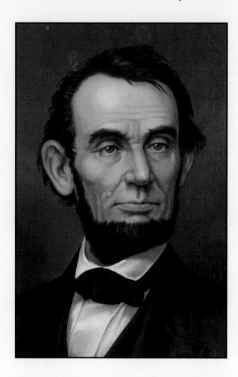

Today, President Abraham Lincoln (1809–1865) is revered by Americans for his leadership in preserving the Union during the dark days of the Civil War.

died and almost an equal number were wounded. Beyond this, large areas of the South came out of the war in desperate shape. Some places in the Deep South did not return to prosperity for decades. But the single most profound change brought about by the war was the freedom of 4 million African Americans.

The American Civil War changed the nature of warfare. Before 1861, most Americans had experienced either limited warfare or none at all, and very few of them had ever been dislocated or orphaned as a result of war. When the war ended in 1865, Americans had introduced to the world the concept of total war, meaning the relentless pursuit of the enemy and the attempt to break the enemy's ability to resist.

Finally, the Civil War remade the image of the United States. Before the war, the nation was a loose-knit confederation of states, with people living in the various sections—North, South, and West—having very different interests. After 1865, the United States truly became a single nation, with the Union—exemplified by the federal government in Washington, D.C.—taking precedence over the individual states.

TEXT-DEPENDENT QUESTIONS

1. Who was the first major Union leader to view desolate Richmond in April 1865?

2. What is the name of the town, or postal village, where Robert E. Lee surrendered?

3. Most of us know that John Wilkes Booth shot President Lincoln. What type of family did Booth come from?

RESEARCH PROJECT

Find out how many towns and cities around the United States are named for President Lincoln.

CHRONOLOGY

1820   Congress passes the Missouri Compromise, by which Maine is partitioned from Massachusetts and admitted to the Union as a free state. Missouri is admitted as a slave state, and it is declared that all lands in the former Louisiana Territory north of latitude 36°30' will be free.

1845   The United States annexes Texas and admits it to the Union as a slave state.

1846   The Mexican War begins.

1848   The United States wins the Mexican War, forcing Mexico to cede a vast territory that will become the states of California, Nevada, Utah, Arizona, and New Mexico.

1850   The Compromise of 1850 is passed. Its components include admission of California as a free state and passage of the Fugitive Slave Act.

1854   The passage of the Kansas-Nebraska Act introduces popular sovereignty as a way to determine whether a new territory will have slavery. This leads to violence between pro-slavery and anti-slavery factions in Kansas.

1860   Abraham Lincoln is elected president; on December 20, South Carolina votes to secede from the Union.

1861   Mississippi, Florida, Alabama, Georgia, Louisiana, and Texas join South Carolina to form the Confederate States of America. On April 12, Confederate batteries begin bombarding Fort Sumter in Charleston Harbor. On July 21, the Union Army is defeated at Bull Run/Manassas.

1862 In February, Union forces under Ulysses S. Grant capture Fort Henry and Fort Donelson in Tennessee. USS *Monitor* and CSS *Virginia* battle in March. At Antietam in September, Union forces stop the Confederates in the bloodiest one-day battle of the war. The Army of the Potomac under General Ambrose Burnside suffers a terrible defeat at Fredericksburg in December.

1863 On January 1, Abraham Lincoln issues the Emancipation Proclamation. The Confederate Army of Northern Virginia defeats Union forces at Chancellorsville, but suffers a major blow with the death of General Thomas "Stonewall" Jackson. The Army of the Potomac turns back a Confederate invasion of Pennsylvania at Gettysburg in early July. The siege of Vicksburg ends with a Union victory on July 4.

1864 In March, Ulysses S. Grant is placed in command of all Union troops. General William T. Sherman's army captures Atlanta in September and begins its "march to the sea." Abraham Lincoln is re-elected president in November. The Confederate army in Tennessee is essentially destroyed by General George H. Thomas at the Battle of Nashville in December.

1865 The Union Army captures Richmond, the Confederate capital. Robert E. Lee surrenders his Army of Northern Virginia on April 9 at Appomattox Court House. Abraham Lincoln is shot on April 14 and dies the next morning. The remaining Confederate forces surrender in May, and the Civil War ends.

CHAPTER NOTES

p. 12: "Look men! There stands …" Barnard Elliott Bee, quoted in Bevin Alexander, *How the South Could Have Won the Civil War: The Fatal Errors that Led to Confederate Defeat* (New York: Crown, 2007), p. 23.

p. 18: "No terms except an unconditional surrender …" Ulysses S. Grant, quoted in James M. McPherson, "Ulysses S. Grant," *American National Biography*, vol. 9 (New York: Oxford University Press, 1999), p. 417.

p. 37: "We here highly resolve …" Abraham Lincoln, "Gettysburg Address," November 19, 1863. Available online at http://www.abrahamlincolnonline.org/lincoln/speeches/gettysburg.htm

p. 40: "He was to go for Lee …" William T. Sherman, quoted in David Alan Johnson, *Decided on the Battlefield: Grant, Sherman, Lincoln and the Election of 1864.* (New York: Prometheus Books, 2012), p. 45.

p. 52: "Let 'em up easy." Abraham Lincoln, quoted in John C. Waugh, *Lincoln and the War's End* (Carbondale: Southern Illinois University Press, 2014), p. 90.

p. 53: "Thus ever to tyrants!" John Wilkes Booth, quoted in Terry Alford, *Fortune's Fool: The Life of John Wilkes Booth* (New York: Oxford University Press, 2015), p. 246.

FURTHER READING

Brands, H. W. *The Man Who Saved the Union: Ulysses Grant in War and Peace*. New York: Doubleday, 2012.

Crompton, Samuel Willard. *The Handy Civil War Answer Book*. Canton, Mich.: Visible Ink Press, 2014

Detweiler, M. David. *The Civil War: The Story of the War with Maps*. Mechanicsburg, PA: Stackpole Books, 2014.

Gwynne, S. C. *Rebel Yell: The Violence, Passion, and Redemption of Stonewall Jackson*. New York: Scribner, 2014.

O'Reilly, Bill. *Lincoln's Last Days: The Shocking Assassination That Changed America Forever*. New York: Henry Holt, 2012.

Thompson, Ben. *Guts and Glory: The American Civil War*. New York: Little, Brown, 2014.

INTERNET RESOURCES

http://www.civilwar150.si.edu

> The Civil War 150th Anniversary (the Smithsonian Institution)

http://www.civilwar.org/battlefields/

> Saving America's Civil War Battlefields (The Civil War Trust)

http://www.usflag.org

> Old Glory—The Flag of the United States of America

http://www.biography.com/people/

> Biographies of Many Civil War Leaders

INDEX

Numbers in ***bold italics*** refer to captions.

SERIES GLOSSARY

blockade—an effort to cut off supplies, war material, or communications in a particular area, by force or the threat of force.

guerrilla warfare—a type of warfare in which a small group of combatants, such as armed civilians, use hit-and-run tactics to fight a larger and less mobile traditional army. The purpose is to weaken an enemy's strength through small skirmishes, rather than fighting pitched battles where the guerrillas would be at a disadvantage.

intelligence—the analysis of information collected from various sources in order to provide guidance and direction to military commanders.

logistics—the planning and execution of movements by military forces, and the supply of those forces.

salient—a pocket or bulge in a fortified line or battle line that projects into enemy territory.

siege—a military blockade of a city or fortress, with the intent of conquering it at a later stage.

tactics—the science and art of organizing a military force, and the techniques for using military units and their weapons to defeat an enemy in battle.